Conquering The Emotional
Roller Coaster
Of Entrepreneurship

Conquering The Emotional Roller Coaster Of Entrepreneurship

Kindra Dionne

Tracee –
Thank you For your
Courage & strength. Thank you
For inspiring me to write. Thank you
For leading by example. Thank you
For paving the way so that the
Rest of us have a path to
Follow.

Kindra

KINDRA DIONNE

Dedication

This book is dedicated a every dreamer who is passionate, purposed, perseverant but yet paused.

Contents

INTRODUCTION

When you begin the journey of entrepreneurship, your mind enters a space that is filled with emotional highs and lows. I know this space all too well. I took up residency here in this emotional cycle for years while I contemplated the idea of entrepreneurship. My feelings about starting a business raced in a loop of excitement and terror, like a runaway roller coaster ride at an amusement park. I realized that the looping was in my mind and it was created by my thoughts and fears about entrepreneurship. The only way to make the looping stop was to take my limiting thoughts captive so that I could finally conquer the, risky yet thrilling, emotional roller coaster of entrepreneurship.

Far too few people speak candidly about the emotional side of entrepreneurship. When we think about the profile of an entrepreneur we think of bravery, boldness, and fearlessness. To transparently share emotions seems weak. To admit that boundless emotional energy is the real culprit for your failure to launch is embarrassing. I believe that more entrepreneurs need to share the truth, about what the experience of starting a business actually feels like. By doing so, we can facilitate the breaking of emotional strongholds, that are keeping aspiring entrepreneurs locked into the seat of their comfort zone, and out of the marketplace.

If someone had explained to me the concepts and ideas that I am about to share with you, I probably would have started my business years ago. People are not the only thing that perishes because of lack of knowledge. Business ideas will also perish in the hands of an unknowledgeable entrepreneur. I believe that it is through our collective experience and willingness to share that we are able to impact generations and contribute innovation to the future of our culture, community, country, and our world.

My goal in writing this book is to ensure mission-driven entrepreneurs enter the marketplace with excellence. This means, if you are an aspiring entrepreneur with the desire to start a business that makes a dollar and a difference, this book is for you. If the only thing standing between you and your first paying customer (that is not a bestie or a relative) is some undealt with emotion, this book is for you. And if you are willing to start the business despite what you may 'feel' like at the present moment, this book is definitely for you.

I always knew I was different. My favorite game to play as a kid was Store. My favorite toy was a plastic cash register, and my favorite things to sketch were products that I could sell in my store. When grownups would ask what I wanted to be when I grew up, my answer was always a businesswoman. The deep desire for entrepreneurship has been burning inside of me since birth. I never wanted to do any regular kid stuff. I wanted to become a young CEO.

My very first business venture was a babysitting service I launched when I was in the fourth grade. I created hand-drawn flyers and business cards to share with the ladies at church. I created activity curriculums to keep the kids engaged, which were really lists of games and other fun things we could do. I created client data sheets to keep track of each kids' personal preferences and emergency contact information, all handwritten with a variety of multi-colored scented markers. And I created a financial ledger to keep track of how much each family paid and any outstanding invoices in my black-and-white composition notebook. Over time, I added services like hair braiding and beading, arts and crafts, and overnight childcare for an additional fee.

By middle school, I ventured into retail. I ran a small convenience store out of my backpack. My top sellers were five-piece packs of bubble gum, lollipops with gum in the middle, and cinnamon-flavored candies that could set your mouth on fire and break your teeth at the same time. This venture was sustained by the adrenaline rush of trying not to get caught by the teachers and supply-and-demand created by my selection of the most popular flavors. I kept track of my weekly sales, and I would ride my bike to the nearby dollar store with a percentage of my weekly profits to restock my supplies every weekend.

In high school, I created a hair braiding salon for men and boys. This business was extremely successful because cornrowed hairstyles were wildly popular, thanks in part to professional athletes and musicians. I had appointments booked every evening after school and on Saturday mornings. I kept this business going even when I went off to college, and I added roller sets and hair perms for girls on campus.

Unbridled passion and entrepreneurial ambition kept me distracted from the trauma and drama of my homelife. My mother was an absolutely amazing woman. She had the sweetest heart and a smile that could light up the room. She was fun, charming, and she loved to dance. Her entire career was spent working as a nurse and serving others. Despite all of her amazing qualities, being raised by her was really hard. What most people didn't know was my mother struggled with mental illness, including depression, anxiety, and suicidal thoughts while battling an alcohol addiction. It's not easy to talk about, but it's true.

I struggled to share about my mother's challenges in this book because she passed away when I was seventeen. She was in her early forties and didn't have a chance to finish living out her own story. I realized that in order for you to fully understand the emotional roller coaster of my entrepreneurial journey, you have to get a sneak peek into my past. My mother did the absolute best she could to provide a great life for me. I could see how hard she fought to keep her illness and addiction from interfering with her life and parenting.

Throughout this book I will share how homelessness, financial insecurity, and being taken into the custody of child protective services multiple times created the underlying fear of taking the big entrepreneurial leap.

Entrepreneurship was never scary to me until the day I found out I was pregnant. I was only seventeen years old. Owning my own business went from a passionate pastime to a back-burner dream because I was determined to not become another teenage mom statistic. I was determined to make my daughter proud and to be the mother to her I needed for myself. The idea of business ownership went from exhilarating to terrifying. The risk of not being financially stable was unnerving for me.

It's amazing how quickly the thing that once fueled my passion turned into an accelerant to fan the flames of my fear. I settled for the world's suggestion that the only way to succeed in life was to get a good education, then a good job, and work until you die. I followed this path for about fifteen years until I decided to step away from my job in economic development and to start my own business development consulting firm.

As a consultant, I serve aspiring entrepreneurs, small businesses, and mid-sized companies, working directly with the CEOs and C-suite executives. At the beginning of every consultation, I like to check in with my clients by asking them to answer one simple question, "Tell me something new and good." Through countless consultations, I began to notice a common thread among the responses to my question. I noticed that everyone experiences emotional highs, lows, twists, and turns as entrepreneurs. No one is exempt. Our emotions are not always the easiest topic to discuss, especially in a business meeting, but it is important to have a safe space to share honestly. During the sessions I also offer my clients "Thoughts for Consideration" instead of telling them what to do. Throughout this book I will do the same for you. I have intentionally included questions that are designed to prompt thought. I would like for you to write your thoughts in the spaces provided as you work your way through each chapter.

Developing an awareness of how my thoughts and emotions impacted my ability to start a business has allowed me to move forward into growing and scaling my Business

Development Consulting Firm. I am so blessed to be able to share my experiences and lessons learned with you in hopes this book gives you the reassurance of knowing you are not alone on the emotional roller coaster of entrepreneurship. I hope the examples and recommendations in this book will spark new thoughts and ideas to move you beyond being emotionally stuck.

Our human nature won't allow us to experience life without emotion. I offer this book to you as a resource to ensure you have tools and a process for developing healthy thoughts for starting your business. With that, I ask that you please secure yourself safely in your seat, keep your hands on your book at all times, and enjoy the read.

5 TIPS TO MAXIMIZE THIS BOOK

(1)   Remain open to the idea that your thoughts have the power to influence your emotions.

(2)   Embrace the suggestion that every emotion that you feel is normal, valid, and real.

(3)   Challenge the "when the time is right" mindset and allow inspiration from this book to guide your creative flow.

(4)   Explore your limits and go beyond your barriers to uncover any underlying emotions that may be in your way.

(5)   Treat this book like your personal permission slip to feel the fear and begin your entrepreneurial journey anyway!

Conquering The Emotional Roller Coaster of Entrepreneurship

PART ONE: CLIMBING INTO THE FRONT SEAT OF THE RIDE

CHAPTER ONE:

EXCITED AND READY TO RIDE

I was more excited than a kid with a new outfit and a fresh pair of shoes on the first day of school to start my business. My big day was finally here, and it was the best feeling in the world. This would be the day I finally got to announce to the world I was open for business. It was literally a dream come true because the idea of actually being an entrepreneur had been in my head for so long, I had convinced myself it was real. My business was a living, breathing, properly structured entity with the official documents to verify its legitness. If I had to describe what it felt like to have an actual business and to finally be a business owner in one word, it would be EXCITING (in all caps). The only thing that was missing was my confidence. I had one hundred percent strategy and zero percent confidence.

How does that even happen? You see, creating a plan and working that plan completely has never been my issue. I can build and create the most amazing business models and operations plan you could ever imagine. Anxiety, guilt, fear, doubt, procrastination, and limiting beliefs would hold me in a vice grip so tight that even after the foundation of a strong business had been strategically laid, nothing would happen. Transformational services would go unused, awe-inspiring workshops would go unfacilitated, game-changing products would go unsold, and liberating books would go unwritten.

Eight times I started a business, each one better than the last. Six times I made it to opening day and failed to launch because I allowed fear to talk me out of it. Four times I had a handful of customers whom I served remarkably well, but I was too afraid to let anyone else know I was open for business. Two times I enlisted the help of a business partnership, hoping the combination of my strategy and work ethic would pair well with their confidence and salesmanship. Then one day, the never-ending emotional roller coaster I was stuck on was closed for maintenance. This meant on this day, there would be no more endless rotation or death-defying loops, twists, or unexpected emotional drops. One time, I was able to exit the emotional roller coaster of entrepreneurship. And this time, I was able to start and successfully run a business that ensured mission-driven entrepreneurs entered the marketplace with excellence so they could make a dollar and a difference.

I grew up in Richmond, Virginia, not too far from a huge amusement park. All winter long, advertising for the latest and greatest rides would run on every commercial break on every channel. I remember watching the commercials with eager anticipation of the park's opening weekend. I remember so many conversations with friends in school about the newest roller coaster and the groups of friends who would plan trips to the park to experience the thrill ride together. On opening weekend, the parking lot would be overflowing with park-goers scrambling for a spot near the gate. Everyone was equally excited to check out the brand-new rides. My friends and I would meet at the park with our season pass in hand, skip the ticketing lines, and head straight to the entry gate. Once inside, we would do everything in our power to dodge the park paparazzi who try to take your picture for the little keychain thing and run directly to the line for the newest roller coaster.

Completely unfazed by the sign that clearly told us the wait time from that point was an hour and forty-five minutes, my friends and I claimed our spot in line. Our excitement grew in intensity as we inched our way in the heat and in the sun toward the coaster station. In line, we talked to everyone around us, sharing our coaster-riding war stories and making recommendations on what we should try next. I remember looking over my shoulder and noticing we were next up to select our riding lane. I was perfectly fine selecting a car somewhere near the center of the train, but at the insistence of my friends we made our way to the very front of the ride. My stomach in knots and heart pounding, I volunteered to step into the ride first. My excitement quickly shifted to nervousness as I watched the smiling faces in the car in front of us transition from glee to terror as the train blasted out of the station to ascend the first hill. The gates opened, and it was our turn to step into the car. After spending nearly two hours waiting, it was finally our time.

Would you believe me if I told you that after coming all this way, I made eye contact with the attendant, located the exit gate, and stepped out onto the other side? I was too afraid to go through with it. I allowed fear to talk me out of the opportunity to experience something new. The walk down the exit ramp felt longer than the wait in line. A rush of embarrassment, disappointment, and hurt came over me. After all that build-up, I didn't follow through. I didn't know whether to go back to get in line and try again or to walk over to the carousel in the kiddie park so I could self-soothe. I simply reverted to my comfort zone and stuck to the rides with only the twists and turns I had committed to memory. There was no thrill. There was no risk. And there was certainly no real reward.

Why did I bother telling you this deeply personal and totally embarrassing roller-coaster story? Because it is the exact same sequence of emotions I felt when I started my first business.

When starting a business, there is no shortage of excitement. You work your day job for eight to ten hours, then you spend about the same amount of time building your business in anticipation of the freedom and flexibility that entrepreneurship promises. The development time to build the business may feel like a temporary sacrifice for long-term reward. Along the way, you will meet plenty of amazing people who are on a similar journey. The people who started out as strangers end up becoming strategic connections who share insights to help achieve your goal.

Thoughts and feelings like doubt and discouragement then creep in, leveraging the energy created by excitement and using it as a positive source of momentum to help you to rise above the challenges you face. The energy created by excitement can be positive or negative. Positive energy produces growth and forward motion. It is magnetic, it is kinetic, and it inspires action. Negative energy creates the opposite effect, making it feel impossible to gain any momentum. It is often confused with procrastination because your desire is so strong, but your confidence is weak, therefore you do nothing.

When you start a business, be it your first time or the thirtieth time, you have to allow your excitement to carry you all the way through to the end. Just like riding a roller coaster, you will feel a myriad of emotions. These emotions are all driven by excitement and adrenaline, and at some point, the topsy-turvy portion of the journey will end. Trust me, when you finally do muster up the courage to see your launch through, you will enjoy the bragging rights that come with conquering the biggest, baddest, and scariest part of starting a business. See it through the twists, turns, and unexpected drops during the initial launch. Don't give up too soon.

Making the decision to launch is the beginning of the waiting process that's necessary to fully develop the foundation of a strong business. Choosing your lane is the process of clearly identifying how you want to introduce your products or services to the market. This is the part where you distinguish yourself and your business from similarly situated businesses that offer similar products and services. A made-up mind, a willing spirit, and the physical effort to do the work is what locks in your commitment to start the journey of business ownership. The commitment you make by taking deliberate actions is fueled by excitement. The energy produced by excitement is what gets the business moving in the right direction. As you begin your entrepreneurial journey, you may be met with an obstacle that appears insurmountable, but don't be discouraged. The resistance you feel is a normal part of the process of overcoming. It is important to ignore the magnetic pull of your comfort zone in order to forge ahead.

Hold on to the knowledge that you are heading in the right direction and you have what it takes to rise above. This builds strength, courage, and character. As you adjust to your new mental strength, remember there are people watching you. Some of the people are supporters cheering you on. A few are spectators who are scared to start their own business, so they are watching to see if anything happens to you first. And you will always have one or two onlookers eagerly waiting for something to go wrong so they can say, "I told you so." Put your blinders on to these people, and do your best to smile. This is your moment, not theirs. Focus on your journey, and make lasting memories along the way.

Remember, nothing will go according to plan, so you have to remain flexible and adaptable, especially early on. When your business starts rolling at a steady pace, allow the energy created by excitement to carry you through the unpredictability of what lies ahead. Take note of the lessons you learn along the way to reduce the element of surprise when launching your next venture and to help others. Most entrepreneurs start more than one business, and their current business can pivot and evolve into new and exciting ventures.

Entrepreneurship is the most exciting and beautifully terrifying thing I have ever done. Embrace the fact that you will experience a lot of emotions on this journey and that's natural and very normal. Don't allow yourself to get caught in an emotional cycle that keeps you from moving forward. Use the energy created by excitement to your advantage. Excitement makes you bold, brave, and boundless if you let it.

A FEW THOUGHTS FOR YOUR CONSIDERATION

When was the last time you allowed fear to keep you from starting something new?

_____

_____

_____

_____

List the top five emotions you felt or currently feel about starting and growing your business.

1. _____

2. _____

3. _____

4. _____

5. _____

What valuable lessons have you learned from your entrepreneurial journey?

_____

_____

_____

_____

If you had your initial launch to do again, what would you do differently?

_____

_____

_____

_____

CHAPTER TWO:

INSPIRATION IS NOT ENOUGH

I like to think of myself as a life-long learner. Investing in my own professional development is important to my growth as a business owner so I try to attend at least three conference each year. The very next purchase I would make after buying a ticket to a conference is a brand-new notebook. *Inspiration guaranteed* may as well be added to each ticket because I knew I would leave each event with pages upon pages of notes all inspired by the speakers on stage and breakout room facilitators. The feeling of enthusiasm and insight I gained always sparked an outpouring of creative new ideas and made me want to grow to a higher level in life and business. I can honestly admit I'm totally addicted to the mental stimulation and the adrenaline-boosting rush of brilliance that comes from learning something new.

When I was a kid, I spent a lot of time with my grandmother. She was by far the busiest and most active woman I have ever met. I remember she made a canvas bag for me with a legal pad, pens and markers, a book, and snacks to keep me occupied while she would attend conferences, meetings, and events. I remember sitting quietly in the back of the room drawing pictures and writing stories. As I got older, the conference organizers would remember me and give me little jobs to do like handing out badges, conference programs, and even ushering guest speakers to their green rooms. I was hooked. In time, I began to listen to what was being shared from the main stage, and I would write notes on the things that inspired me. My grandmother would always have a car full of ladies who would travel with us to these events, and they loved to hear me share my take-aways during the ride home. I eventually grew up and became youth chapter president for some of the organizations, and I even had multiple opportunities to speak on stage. Early exposure developed my imagination, creativity, and desire to learn and draw inspiration from the stories of others.

Creativity without inspiration leads to frustration and an endless cycle of stagnation. The best thing an aspiring or early stage entrepreneur can do is learn to find inspiration everywhere. Inspiration will awaken your ingenuity and expand your thinking to new possibilities by allowing you to rise above your ordinary experiences and limits. Inspiration will propel you from procrastination to action and transform the way you view your own potential. People often underestimate the power of inspiration because of its elusive nature. It is hard to define and measure inspiration. Few people have been able to trace the real return on investment (ROI) of inspiration. Most people don't recognize inspiration for what it truly is. Inspiration is a feeling of enthusiasm that comes from someone or something you encountered, which leads you to creative and innovative ideas.

Your thoughts and feelings during the early stages of starting a business can be as topsy-turvy as the loops of a roller coaster. Tapping into multiple sources of inspiration can empower you to become a natural source of energy to fuel your positive and creative thinking. Build your own inspirational reserve by intentionally establishing an idea community of successful people and resources to keep you motivated to grow. This is key to turning a dream into an action-oriented goal.

Finding inspiration is about so much more than an emotional burst of enthusiasm. It is also developing a tool kit of models, methods, and mindsets to help you launch and run a successful business. Inspiration can also be about identifying useful information and resources to move your idea farther along. Leveraging the right sources of inspiration can be a game changer for your business. Let us explore some ideas and concepts for finding business inspiration, how to use inspiration to launch and grow, and ways to convert the energy created by inspiration into fuel to develop and execute a plan of action for business success.

The energy created by inspiration makes it realistic and possible to do things we otherwise would not. There is a magical transfer that happens when you watch someone you admire achieve a goal that is remarkably similar to your own. The inspiration that results from your observation is the motivating factor that moves you to begin or continue to work toward your own business goals. It helps you to create a mental picture of you achieving your goal and leads you into the glorious transition from someone who has an idea to a legitimate entrepreneur.

Thinking about the idea of business ownership is thrilling. Thinking about the steps necessary to start a business is very overwhelming. Some people are more successful in finding an excuse than they are at finding a way. Inspiration can be the excuse remover that pushes you beyond chronic procrastination into the realm of exponential growth.

To build an idea community, you must first be clear on what you would like to accomplish with your business. Next, you need to determine if you already have an idea community you may not be leveraging or if you need to build one to benefit you. As you put your ideas in writing, try to answer the following questions:

An idea community is a professional network of like-minded business owners who inspire you, share valuable resources, serve as accountability partners, and are transparent when it comes to sharing the truth about their own entrepreneurial journey. There is typically no formal structure to your personal idea community, and the members are not actually members. These are people you meet and gravitate toward. Many cities and towns have regular business networking events that offer a great opportunity for you to make intentional connections with individuals who are currently doing or who have successfully done the things you aspire to do. Social media has created a platform for virtual groups and online communities for business owners. Choose your favorite platform, and search for groups that are focused on entrepreneurship, business ownership, or other topics related to starting a business that inspires you. Having a broad network is so valuable to your business growth and consistent inspiration. Developing a relationship with a business mentor also comes with its fair share of perks. A personal connection to someone who is invested in helping you succeed decreases the likelihood of procrastination and increases your drive to complete your task lists.

As you are building your idea community and finding sources of inspiration, don't underestimate the value of a good book. The inspiring stories of other entrepreneurs can help set your mind at ease and usher in a fresh perspective for overcoming obstacles. Reading about innovative businesses and awe-inspiring entrepreneurs is a great way to keep inspiration at your fingertips.

Without action, inspiration is no more than decorative notebook filler. Each inspired goal must be backed by deliberate and consistent action in order to progress from idea to lucrative business. To harness the energy created by inspiration and use it as fuel for action, your goals must be written down. This is one of the easiest things you can do to build momentum for your launch. Writing out your inspired goals helps you to clear out the distracting brain clutter, organize your thoughts, and break larger tasks into manageable steps.

Consider signing up for workshops, classes, or conferences. These educational events can build your knowledge and skills while introducing new ways to put your inspiration into action. These events are also a great way to make connections with likeminded people who could be added to your idea community. Learning together brings unity, discovery, and accountability, which are valuable for growing a business. There are few people who truly understand the emotional roller coaster of entrepreneurship quite like another entrepreneur. Creating connections with fellow entrepreneurs forms a partnership for accountability, a resource with whom to share productivity tips, and someone with whom to celebrate large and small victories. No one stays inspired one hundred percent of the time. Inspiration has hills and valleys, twists and turns, and the occasional unexpected drop just like a roller coaster. Keep your business inspiration close by so you can refuel, re-energize, and refocus along the way. You may decide to keep your inspired ideas on a vision board, in a picture journal, or maybe even in a special folder on your computer. No matter where you decide to keep your inspiration, make sure it is accessible for the moments you feel less than stellar.

A FEW THOUGHTS FOR YOUR CONSIDERATION

What is your launch plan for your business?

_____

_____

_____

_____

What like-minded individuals inspire you and why?

_____

_____

_____

_____

Who do you consider a mentor?

_____

_____

_____

_____

Why do you need a mentor?

_____

_____

_____

_____

What books or resources can you use to inspire and motivate you?

_____

_____

_____

_____

CHAPTER THREE:

POWERED BY AMBITION

There is a huge difference between saying you're going to start a business and actually starting one. Interestingly, many ambitious individuals with an entrepreneurial spirit speak about their business as if it's already established and thriving, even when it's in the concept stage. This is actually an exceptionally good thing to do. The truth is, if you aren't convinced your business can and will exist someday, it will be much harder to actually create and launch it. You have to speak about your business as if you're already generating revenue. Doing so will cause your mind, body, and willpower to come into agreement, and soon, you'll be able to manifest what you've envisioned and professed. Your thoughts become your actions, your actions become your habits, and your habits create your results. It takes a bold and ambitious person to conceptualize and launch a business.

Let's go a little deeper to develop a better understanding of what ambition truly is and how to use the energy created by ambition to move your business forward.

Ambition is the spark that's produced when your desire to achieve collides with your internal drive to take action. That spark ignites your tenacity and determination and keeps you going during the times others may have quit. The spark of ambition reflects the light that shines brightly in your eyes whenever you speak about your business or your idea. Someone who strives to reach their goals and who demonstrates perseverance and determination without giving up is the definition of ambition personified.

Ambition often feels like approaching a roller coaster with terror and excitement both dancing in a sensual yet emotional tango in the pit of your stomach as you weave your way through the line to board the ride.

Ambition is a key driver behind any entrepreneurial success. It's the emotion that sustains you and nudges you to keep going when your business faces challenges. Ambition fills in the gaps when talent and resources are low or non-existent. In entrepreneurship, ambition will inspire you to make things happen instead of waiting for things to happen. Positive energy created by ambition leads to entrepreneurial achievement and business growth. Like most things, ambition has an ugly side too. Excessive ambition can create negative energy, which leads to burnout, frustration, and costly mistakes.

Starting a business is an ambitious decision. I remember when I decided to launch my business consulting firm. I was working a full-time job during the day, a part-time job at night, and dabbling in a multi-level marketing business, all while carrying the brunt of my family's financial burden. My marriage was falling apart, and nothing at the time seemed to be working in my favor. I had always had the desire to be an entrepreneur, and I knew I would be successful if I could muster up enough courage to simply start.

In August 2017, my desire to be an entrepreneur had a collision with my drive to change the direction in which my life was headed, and I began to take action. My ambition wouldn't allow me to use "I don't have enough time" as an excuse to not build my business. Each night, after working my part-time job, I would focus and complete one task to move my business forward. For the first few weeks, I concentrated on establishing the legal structure. I got my employer identification number one night. The next night, I registered my business with my state corporation commission. The next night, I completed my zoning and business license process, and I continued in this manner until everything was done.

It sounds simple, right? Wrong. There was nothing simple about it. I remember being so exhausted once that I tripped and fell down a flight of stairs while trying to make it to the computer in the basement to work on my business. I sat there at the bottom of the steps in pain physically and emotionally, crying and praying my efforts wouldn't be in vain. I remember spending a full week on a do-it-yourself website trying to create something that looked like I had a professional build it. Night one, I created the home page. Night two, the About page. Night three, the Services page, and I followed that workflow until the tasks were complete.

My ambition wouldn't allow me to stop. I was working for something far more satisfying than the temporary relief of sleep. I had to keep going. By October 2017, I turned in my two-week notice to quit my full-time job. I was terrified. And after two months of incremental and consistent effort, I was ready for the soft opening of my business. I was so proud of what I had achieved. Nothing about the process was easy, but every part of the process was worth it.

In February 2018, I held my official ribbon cutting. And one month after that, my divorce proceedings began. Running my company as a single mother, solopreneur, and soon-to-be two-time divorcee with zero dollars of a financial safety net was terrifying. I don't recommend it. My faith and my work ethic paired so eloquently with my ambition during this transitional season in my life. I knew if I remained steadfast and focused on growth, the toughest parts of my journey would soon pass on by, and I would be well on my way to achieving the business of which I dreamed.

Ambition is not a one size fits all. There are at least five levels and types of ambitious entrepreneurs.

Level One: The Wantrepreneur. This entrepreneur's ambition is in dialect only. They talk a good game and may even be actively involved in the ideation process of creating a business, but they've never completed any official formation actions. These entrepreneurs will quickly walk away from their business idea at the first sign of hardship or struggle.

Level Two: The Hustlerpreneur. This entrepreneur is fueled by the ambitious desperation that creates a mindset of "this is my only option." They are willing to start the business now and learn how to run it later. These entrepreneurs are ambitious enough to start four or five micro-businesses or side hustles at one time. None of the side businesses produce enough to sustain the entrepreneur, but the combination of the revenue produced by all of their micro-businesses generates just enough to make ends meet.

Level Three: The Workerpreneur. This entrepreneur's true ambition is to never work for anyone else again. Essentially, they own their job. They have no staff and no desire to ever hire a staff. On paper they're business owners, but in actuality what they have is a job, and they double as the employer. The driving force behind their ambition is to earn as much as, or slightly more than, other professionals with a similar title.

Level Four: The Dreamerpreneur. This entrepreneur is remarkably ambitious as long as they remain focused on achieving the life of their dreams. They have an undeniable ability to visualize all aspects of their dream life. They create vision boards filled with the finer things in life and images of the lifestyle they aspire to live. Their ambition remains strong until they have achieved their goals and then they mellow into maintenance. Their focus shifts to maintaining the life they have created and not really moving beyond that point.

Level Five: The Execupreneur. This entrepreneur is all action and little discussion. Their ambition is fueled by their last big win. They are not afraid to invest in talented team members to advance their business pursuits. As their ambition grows, their company grows too. They are confident in their business decisions and are unafraid to take risks. Their growth is exponential, and their success is compounded by their consistency, resilience, and effort.

Converting entrepreneurial ambition to energy is easy, but it is your responsibility to use it. Ambition is useless without deliberate action. Thinking about starting is one thing. Actually, starting is something different. Thinking about growth is great. Working toward growth produces desirable results.

A FEW THOUGHTS FOR YOUR CONSIDERATION

Using the space below, write the story you share with others about your business or business idea.

_____

_____

_____

_____

_____

_____

_____

_____

Briefly describe the emotions you feel when you share your business concept with others.

_____

_____

_____

_____

On a scale of 1-5 how would you rate your current level of ambition towards starting your business?

Not Ambitious **1** **2** **3** **4** **5** Highly
At All   Ambitious

What level and type of entrepreneur are you? Why?

_____

_____

PART TWO: ASCENDING THE FIRST BIG

CHAPTER FOUR:

ENTREPRENEURIAL PERFORMANCE ANXIETY

Entrepreneurial performance anxiety as the fear of doing business in front of others. It is the strong mental desire to act, met by an unintended physical resistance, or extreme procrastination. It can be physically, mentally, and emotionally frustrating. It can feel like your life's calendar, biological clock, and your heart's intentions are all out of sync when it comes to starting or growing your business. Even when you physically sit in front of your computer to work, your mind goes blank, and you are easily distracted by shiny objects and non-essential tasks. Entrepreneurial Performance Anxiety can literally feel like an invisible force is physically holding you in place and preventing you from moving and even thinking clearly.

Causes

The idea of starting a business isn't something we just wake up one morning and decide to do. Most people have an idea they toss around in their mind for a bit, and when they're ready, they start taking steps to bring their business idea to life. Anxiety and feelings of nervous energy don't kick in until you start taking action to do something with your business idea. Performing a routine task like creating an email account or selecting a name for your business can trigger entrepreneurial performance anxiety, simply because of the amount of pressure we put on ourselves to create something amazing on the first try. Feelings of uneasiness and restlessness slowly enter into your mind and body as you try to process how you'll balance launching your business and getting all the work done with all of your other responsibilities.

Sharing your business idea with others also makes you feel extremely vulnerable. It can also leave you feeling open and totally exposed. It is very natural to be worried or concerned about what other people think of your business idea. You never truly know how the people in your life will respond to you starting a business. I call these people your committee of peers. Often their response may actually be a projection of their own fears, doubts, or insecurities, and not a true representation of their feelings toward you. This type of response can lead to negative thoughts and feelings that trigger performance anxiety.

On the contrary, some people you share ideas with may totally surprise you and offer sincere support, encouragement, and really help you to launch and grow your business. Even though this type of response can lead to positive thoughts, it can still trigger a level of anxiety. You are now facing the pressure to exceed the expectations of your supporters and make everyone proud. I call this a performance for your committee of peers.

Feeling anxiety and nervous energy isn't a bad thing. It's your body's way of letting you know it's time to start building and moving your business. You must learn to use this energy to your advantage. A certain amount of nervousness and anxiety can actually help you build a solid foundation for your business.

Common Triggers

Understanding the roots or origins of our fears can help us identify the cause of our anxiety. The most common triggers of entrepreneurial performance anxiety originate from five underlying fears:

- **The fear of public speaking.** Glossophobia typically appears when you are expected to speak in front of other people. This fear can prevent you from sharing your idea with potential investors, effectively networking, and even presenting your solution to a prospective client's problem. This fear is a relationship blocker because it is directly connected to effective communication, which is essential to establishing and maintaining value-added relationships.

- **The fear of starting something new.** Neophobia is the fear of anything new. It manifests as the unwillingness to break a routine. Overcoming this fear challenges you to step away from your comfort zone. Building a business can make you extremely uncomfortable because you must be willing to take some risks. If you experience performance anxiety every time you have to make a decision, your anxiety may be rooted in this fear.

- **The fear of rejection.** Social anxiety disorder is the fear of being rejected, judged, or watched by others. This type of anxiety leads to fear that inhibits your ability to let the world know your business exists. This fear makes us think things like, *Who am I to start this business? There are so many people who are better at this than me,* or *Why would someone even buy from me when they can buy from someone else?* Our natural aversion to feelings of hurt and pain can trigger entrepreneurial performance anxiety.

- **The fear of being copied.** Imitation is the highest form of flattery, even in business. Don't allow your fear of someone else "stealing" your idea to keep you out of the marketplace. This fear triggers performance anxiety in such a way that it prevents you from ever starting. Many other business owners will have ideas that are similar to yours, but they don't have you. Understand your unique value proposition and stick to it. Besides, how many burger restaurants can you name? What is the major difference between them? Are they still successful? Exactly.

- **Perfectionism.** This form of anxiety is deeply rooted in the fear of not living up to unrealistic expectations. These expectations are often set by you, as a result of comparing your business idea to someone else's who is likely farther along in the building and development process. This is normal. We set our eyes on the prize and get after it without patiently following the natural growth steps. A farmer doesn't reap a harvest in the same season she plants a seed, so why do you expect windfall profits in the same fiscal quarter you launch? Keep your blinders on, and focus your energy on building your own business, not watching someone else build theirs.

Practical Application

Identify Negative and Limiting Thoughts

It's really hard to change something you can't identify. In order to convert the energy created from entrepreneurial performance anxiety into something useful for your business, you must identify your negative and limiting thoughts. My mentor once told me to add "…and that's exactly what I want" to any negative or limiting thoughts that ran through my mind. Those six simple words were powerful enough to change my perspective on so many things. I'll give you an example. If I were to say, "I probably won't have a lot of customers in my first year of business" that would be a negative and limiting thought. Now let's add my mentor's words to my statement. "I probably won't have a lot of customers in my first year of business, and that's exactly what I want." Adding those six words is like highlighting paragraphs in a good book, it causes the words to stand out. No one wants to have only a few customers in their first year of business, so why do we say things like this? When you find yourself entertaining negative and limiting thoughts identify them by adding "…and that's exactly what I want" to the end and see if the thought is still true. Be gentle with yourself and replace the negative and limiting thought with a positive and productive one.

Proper Perspective Produces Action

Remember, we all have fears. Professionally, you will meet lots of business owners at various levels of success. Never let someone else's success intimidate you. The world is patiently waiting for what you offer. The more you work your business, the more amazing it will become. The efforts of consistently taking small actions daily will have an exponential effect on your business and your confidence.

Talk to a Trusted Mentor, Friend, or Family Member

We all need a safe sounding board. Find someone you trust who will actively listen to you, even if you find yourself talking in circles or saying the same thing over and over.

Sometimes the best way to manage and convert entrepreneurial performance anxiety is to talk it out.

Create a Schedule and Stick to It

Not meeting business growth deadlines can really contribute to entrepreneurial performance anxiety. Planning your work and working your plan is the pathway to productivity. Use your calendar and allocate time weekly to work on your business, then gradually add work time daily until you are spending a few hours each day working on your business. Aim to complete one small task at a time because dedicating your time to get one thing off your plate does better for your business confidence than haphazardly starting multiple tasks you never complete.

Don't Be Afraid to Ask for Help

Just because you believe you can do everything to start your business on your own doesn't mean you should. Set a budget for services that are important but that don't require you to do it alone. For example, there are tons of DIY marketing tools available for you to use. Hiring a professional, who is skilled in marketing, can help your company reach your target customer faster, leading to increased sales, because they are more skilled in this work. Build relationships with other business owners who may be willing to barter services. Be sure to create a healthy boundary around your bartering. Consider adding time limits, specific services, or limiting yourself to two barters per quarter. You're not setting up a booth at a swap meet, you're bringing a new product or service into a competitive business marketplace. You deserve to make money and to be fairly compensated for your work. Always remember that. Also, find a good business consultant or coach who can help you build and stick with a strategy to make significant progress.

Make a Decision

Over the course of a single day, you can and will make thousands of decisions. When it comes to the business you're starting or growing, deciding can feel like an impossible task. Decision fatigue is a real thing, so make it easy on yourself by forgetting about perfection and breaking your big decisions into smaller steps you can easily prioritize.

Get It Done

Entrepreneurial performance anxiety naturally fades when you simply do something. The best way to overcome anxiety is to start and measure your small successes along the way. You must give yourself credit for the accomplishments you achieve. Starting a business isn't easy, but it is possible, and it is worth it. Your business will never be successful if you don't start it.

Closing Thoughts

Repurposed entrepreneurial performance anxiety shows up in your business as confidence, boldness, and excitement. Stomach knots, fear, and anxiety are real, but they don't have to destroy your business. Use the energy created by entrepreneurial performance anxiety to achieve small victories and to accomplish incremental growth, which will lead to sustainable progress. The goal is to grow in confidence with each positive action you take to move your business forward and allow your entrepreneurial performance anxiety to slowly fade.

A FEW THOUGHTS FOR YOUR CONSIDERATION

How has entrepreneurial performance anxiety delayed the launch of your business?

_____

_____

_____

_____

Which underlying fear do you struggle with? How is that impacting your business?

_____

_____

_____

_____

CHAPTER FIVE:

PROCRASTINATION IS NOT LAZINESS

Your reason for procrastination may be much deeper than some surface issue or distraction. Procrastination is the habitual or intentional avoidance or delay of starting or finishing a task despite the potential of negative consequences. Your procrastinatory behavior as a business owner may be linked to your work history. Have you spent years working with overly critical managers, judgmental peers who would rather criticize than help, or in high-pressure environments with low margins for error? Your procrastination habits may be linked to thoughts or memories of your past experiences. These career experiences coupled with your life experiences can create fear, which leads to procrastination in your own business. It's hard to erase years of conditioning that says, "If you make a mistake, there will be negative consequences," but you can't allow it to stop you from trying. Adopting healthy thoughts about yourself, your ability, and your business is the first step to overcoming procrastination and moving your business forward. Psychologically speaking, chronic procrastination may be linked to a more serious mental health concern. This is nothing to be ashamed of nor should you try to cope with this on your own. Reach out to a licensed and trained mental health professional for support. I'm a firm believer and active patient of good mental health.

Owning my own business has always been a dream of mine. I can remember countless stories of my entrepreneurial endeavors, even at an early age. Life, time, and a myriad of experiences planted seeds of fear and self-doubt that eventually made me question whether I could be successful in business ownership. Deep down, I knew all the wonderful benefits that being my own boss would have for my family. I would create vision boards and affirmations to keep my mind on positive thoughts. No matter how badly I wanted to start my own business, I couldn't seem to make any steps in that direction. When it came time to write the business plan, the pen seemed to weigh a thousand pounds. When I tried to articulate my business idea, all words would leave my head. It was as if there were a literal blockage preventing me from taking the necessary action to start my business.

It was in multiple sessions with my therapist that I realized my real issue: I always believed there would be new battles to fight on every level you ascend to in life and business. The size of the battle would be proportionate to the magnitude of the level. I have literally spent my entire life fighting battles, defying odds, and dismantling stereotypes that had been applied to my life, and quite frankly, I was sick and tired of fighting. I knew the intrinsic and extrinsic rewards of life on the level of business owner, but the idea of battling the challenges that came with that level were enough to keep me stuck in procrastination land. My behavior was self-sabotaging and selfish. I wasn't willing to disrupt my personal comfort in order to create a better life for my family. Thousands of aspiring business owners around the world wouldn't be able to achieve the levels they deserve because I was unwilling to fight for my own destiny.

It was in therapy that I realized the idea this "epic battle" that had to be won in order for me to become a business owner existed in my own thoughts. I realized starting the business didn't initiate the battle that would ultimately determine my entrepreneurial fate. It was what I thought about starting a business that initiated the mental warfare, which distracted me from even trying. Therapy taught me to take my thoughts captive and to convert my negative and nonproductive thoughts into positive and productive action. It started with creating a list of the things I believed I needed to do to successfully start my business.

Making a to-do list for your new business is easy. Completing the tasks on your list is not. Your attitude, behavior, circumstances, feelings, situations, and thoughts all play an influential role in how, when, or if you take action. If you want to get through your list and create positive momentum in your business, try using the 3D method of getting through your list. Keep track of the type of tasks you procrastinate over most frequently. Categorize them by one of the three Ds listed below and act accordingly.

1) **Do It Now.** Some tasks are easy to do, which makes them easy not to do. Dedicate time early in your day to tackle the easy stuff first. You'll jump-start your momentum with the satisfaction that comes from checking off a box.

2)   **Delegate** the tasks you can do but you don't need to do personally. Some tasks can be assigned to team members (if you have them) or subcontracted to another business who specializes in that area. An

example of this is creating promotional materials for your grand opening. Just because you know how to do this doesn't mean it's the highest and best use of your time. Hire a freelance graphic designer or a company who specializes in promotional graphics to handle this and other related tasks for you. Your time is better spent building personal connections with prospective customers by personally inviting them as your guest to the event.

3) **Discard** any and all tasks from your list that aren't urgent or necessary for a successful opening day. It's easy to fill your task list with time wasters that feel important but that really aren't. Ask yourself these three questions:

1. Does this add value?

2. What is the immediate consequence of not having this done?

3.   Is this something I want to do or need to do before I can successfully open my business?

Salience is the mischievous first cousin of procrastination. Separately, they can create blind spots that lead to non-productive busyness, which is bad for business. Together, they will wreak havoc on your entrepreneurial mindset and profit potential. Salience in relation to procrastination means to place too much value on what you can see and not enough value on what you can't see. When making business decisions or simply working through your to-do list, it's easy to procrastinate because you aren't thinking about how your decision today might impact you in the future. Your decision is primarily based on how this delay will impact you right now. Stress relief, more free time, and the preservation of your comfort zone help to justify your decision to procrastinate. If you take the time to think beyond the present, you'll begin to see the value in avoiding procrastination.

Looking deeper into time inconsistency can help us to understand why we procrastinate in our business. Time inconsistency is about who you are as decision maker and the actions you take as a result. It assumes there is more than one version of you when it comes to decision making. Each version of you as a decision maker shows up at certain points in time and makes inconsistent choices when your preferences aren't aligned.

Here is an example of how time inconsistency influences attitudes, thoughts, behaviors, and outcomes. The night before a proposal or project is due, some business owners tend to wish they had more time to produce. If the opportunity for a due date extension were presented, those business owners would be willing to pay money for a little more time. If those same business owners were asked at the very beginning if the due date allowed enough time, they might say the date was fine and wouldn't be willing to pay money for an extension. The opportunity is the same in both scenarios however, the decision is being made at different points in time. Procrastination happens when you make decisions based on how you think and feel in the moment without regard for how this may impact you or your business in the future. This is also an example of an empathy gap that can undermine your success.

An empathy gap is a cognitive bias that occurs when you underestimate the influence of your feelings (or lack thereof), emotional reactions, and your instinctive drive on your attitude, behavior, preferences, and thoughts. To illustrate the effect of the empathy gap in entrepreneurship, I want you to think of a time when you watched or heard the story of a business similar to the one you want to start failing or experiencing some unimaginable challenge. Can you feel your chest tighten just thinking about how you would react if this tragic circumstance somehow happened to you? Is the thought of their misfortune somehow becoming your problem, which leads you to procrastination? Cognitive bias influences how we think and can lead to errors in judgment and decision making. It is exceedingly difficult for you as a business owner to predict how you will behave in the future.

In the early stages of business ownership, you will be faced with challenges and obstacles you've never dealt with before. Without any clear indicators or predictions of how your decision to face these obstacles or challenges might affect your business in the future, you may unintentionally slip into a cycle of procrastination. Our natural response is to start asking around to find out how others have handled this particular challenge. We will spend countless hours on the internet searching for clues on what we should decide.

We may even pick up a book to find greater insight and examples on what we should do. All of this is great; however, this procrastination is not due to the lack of ability. This procrastination stems from an underlying fear or insecurity causally linked to perfectionism. Take a moment and ask yourself these three questions:

- What am I really afraid of?

- How do I truly benefit from putting it off?

- Am I actually scared or did someone else tell me it was scary?

If you're honest with yourself, you know business ownership feels equal parts exciting and terrifying. Thoughts of judgment or criticism can lead to feelings of vulnerability, inadequacy, and inexperience. This leads to a paralyzing inability to act or decide, which then results in procrastination.

The energy created by procrastination can feel a lot like anxiety, which can lead to mild depression, low self-esteem, stress, and even actual anxiety if you don't convert the negative thoughts this energy can produce. To convert the energy produced by procrastination into useful energy to move your business forward, you must learn how to shift your thinking in order to structure your work. Here are a few steps to help:

Focus on What You Know

Try not to focus on what you don't know. Be confident in what you do know. Do your best to figure things out. Try and learn from any mistakes you may make along the way. If you get caught up in focusing on what you don't know, it's easy to get distracted into not taking action. Trust me, distractions destroy more businesses than any mistake ever will.

Make Deliberate and Consistent Action

To achieve exponential growth, action must be intentional and frequent. It takes time to see results, so deliberate and consistent steps forward daily will compound and build, leading to a business of which you can be proud.

Review the Lesson and Take Notes

Mistake or success, you must take time to review the outcomes of your actions. The best way to conquer the fear of failure is to do something then analyze your results. Ask yourself, *Am I more afraid of the process or the result?* Write out the process or steps you took and results then make note of what you can do differently in the future.

Build a Bridge and Get Over It

You must master the art of moving on. To stay stuck rehearsing the lines of what went wrong is another form of procrastination. Business ownership has never been the scientific practice of perfection. You can and will hear countless stories of successful businesses who have failed their way forward. You are not exempt from this part of the process. The sooner you accept this truth, the sooner your business will grow.

Procrastination is the arrogant assumption you somehow deserve another opportunity to do what you should have done yesterday. Try to avoid delaying tasks that are easy to complete. You deserve to win at entrepreneurship. Don't give up on yourself or your dream.

A FEW THOUGHTS FOR YOUR CONSIDERATION

What was one key thought that stood out to you in this chapter?

_____

_____

_____

How will understanding the underlying fear or linking event help you to overcome procrastination?

_____

_____

_____

_____

Which of the three steps to move beyond procrastination will you start using right away?

_____

_____

_____

_____

CHAPTER SIX:

GROWING BEYOND THE GRIP OF GUILT

How come no one ever talks about the immense amount of guilt that comes with entrepreneurship?

We always hear about how exciting entrepreneurship is. We hear stories about the freedom that comes with being your own boss. We even share quotes on social media about how entrepreneurs are willing to work eighty hours a week for themselves just to avoid working forty hours a week for someone else, yet you rarely hear anyone speak of the guilt associated with being an entrepreneur. Where does entrepreneurial guilt come from? The beliefs and values your family of origin and community places on working a traditional job and entrepreneurship can contribute to the feeling of guilt. The responsibilities you have to your household can play a role in creating the overwhelming sense of guilt. Also, being constantly misunderstood by people who have never ventured into the wild world of entrepreneurship can also make you feel guilty about your career choice of starting a business.

For me, the idea of walking away from what I believed was a stable income into the riskiest endeavor I had ever taken brought with it an overwhelming sense of guilt. I felt entrepreneur guilt before I ever started my business. Living out my dream of business ownership, setting my schedule, and traveling the world sounded like a good idea. The reality of not knowing how long it would take to turn a profit or how I would pay my bills month after month made me feel guilty about even thinking of quitting my job to start a business. I would look at my child and think, *I can't do this to her. She deserves better than this.*

As I share in this book, my life growing up was filled with so much instability and uncertainty that I never wanted to pass that feeling on to my own family. I was willing to sacrifice my dream in order to make sure everyone else was okay. I never considered the possibility maybe my business would be successful and we would be able to do more than live paycheck to paycheck. Guilt clouded the idea that we could actually enjoy vacations, shopping trips, and other things that didn't require me to walk through stores with the calculator to make sure I didn't bust the budget. Entrepreneur guilt kept me stuck on the tracks even though I knew my dream had the potential to move me and my family forward.

It took years for me to work up the courage to walk away from full-time employment to finally start my business. I literally needed signs, wonders, rainbows, and all sorts of confirming miracles to happen before I could muster up just enough confidence to leap. When I finally started the company, I was truly blessed to have a few customers ready to utilize my services. I had done some preliminary marketing and outreach to announce the opening of my business. The excitement and positive results I saw gave me the assurance I was on track to build a successful business. The adrenaline rush of feeling the exponential growth of my business had me working sixteen to eighteen hours a day seven days a week.

I was unstoppable until one day my body made me stop. I felt dizzy, lethargic, and I had constant headaches. Shocker. I was dehydrated and exhausted, so my doctor recommended I take a few days to rest and properly recover. Although I tried extremely hard to follow the doctor's orders, I lay in bed crying because I felt guilty for not working. When you are raised in an environment where lack is the norm, you constantly feel uneasy about not having enough. My business was my only source of income, and if I didn't work, my family didn't eat. I knew I needed to rest, but I had bills to pay. I was responsible for putting a roof over my family's head, food on our table, and clothing on our backs. That all costs money, which I wasn't making while taking a nap. After two-days of guilt-ridden rest, I was able to return to work, and I still didn't slow down. I actually took on even more projects because I felt like I had to make up for lost time or else. My body kept sending me signs I was consistently ignoring. I gained a tremendous amount of weight, I was getting injured doing the most basic of tasks, and I was an emotional mess, all because I wasn't taking time off to rest. As you may have guessed, my reluctance to step away from my work lead to more time in the recovery bed and not enough time simply relaxing. This time, I finally realized taking a day off was not a day wasted.

I also had to learn and fully accept that taking time off is not the same as being lazy. Taking time off is necessary and nothing to feel guilty about. Taking time off is the healthiest thing you can do for your bottom line. The same guilt that kept me on the clock for an unrealistic number of hours is likely the same reason many entrepreneurs don't make time for days off or vacation.

Four Tips to Eliminate Entrepreneurial Guilt

Surround yourself with like-minded people. Everyone in your life won't fully understand what it's genuinely like to be a full-time entrepreneur. The pressure to blend in can be pretty intense, especially when entrepreneurship makes you stand out. For most people, having endless conversations about the work they do can be a nightmare, but for entrepreneurs, business conversations are energizing and almost therapeutic. You don't have to feel like a conversational drain or a babbling burden on your friends and family who just don't get it if you network and make connections with other entrepreneurs who are also in growth mode.

Align your priorities and your non-negotiables. What are your priorities? What are your non-negotiables? Have you taken time to think about these two things in relation to your business? Utilize your calendar to help you manage your time in such a way that your priorities, non-negotiables, and your business all fit. This is especially helpful if you're a parent. Parental guilt can and will make you stop everything just for your children. As a parent and entrepreneur, you may feel as if you have to choose between being present for your children and building your business. Blocking off family time allows you to schedule time to work on your business around familial commitments. Try to populate your calendar one month at a time, and be sure you add in a few hours for self-care too.

Build a winning team to help carry out your dream. No one is self-made. Surround yourself with people who have natural gifts, professional skills, and time to help you build. This may include dedicated staff, contactors, vendors, interns, volunteers, and friends. Your team needs to be comprised of people you trust with your vision. Delegate the things you can do but don't have to do yourself so you have more time to grow other areas of your business. Having a support system in place reduces any guilty feelings you may feel about having no time because you're doing so much on your own. You don't have to build it alone. Give yourself permission to share the load.

Embrace the word *no*. *No* isn't offensive. *No* is protection. You can't be everything to everyone all of the time. You have to decide if what you're being asked to do aligns with your priorities, non-negotiables, and overall business goals. If not, it's totally appropriate to say no from time to time. Opportunities can be distractions if you aren't careful. When you truly begin the process of growing your business, people will begin to notice you and all the things you are good at. Innocently enough, they may present opportunities that may seem like a natural fit for you. You must develop the courage to say no and resist the temptation to say yes to every opportunity, especially early on in your business.

Guilt and shame are not a good foundation for any relationship, and it is certainly no good for the relationship between you and your business. The energy created by guilt is negative and destructive. It is amazingly easy to get caught up with subconscious thoughts like, *I can't take a break until my business is successful* or *Starting a business will be a burden on my family.* These thoughts will never serve you. Take a moment to reflect on how guilt may have robbed you of your official launch date far too many times. Today is a great day to take those thoughts captive and declare and end to the vicious loop of guilt. You have everything you need to be great.

 # A FEW THOUGHTS FOR YOUR CONSIDERATION

What guilt related issues do you need to address in order to fully realize your entrepreneurial potential?

_____

_____

_____

_____

_____

_____

**PART THREE: TRYING TO IGNORE YOUR
PHOTO BEING TAKEN**

CHAPTER SEVEN: UNDERSTANDING THE PHYSICS OF FEAR

I will never forget when I made the decision to finally take the big leap and leave my job to start my business. It felt like I was at a major crossroads between two critical internal questions—start now or start later? At the time, I felt completely paralyzed by fear. I was afraid to start the business, and I was afraid not to start. Anxiety was the dominate feeling that regulated the pit of my stomach like an endless drop on a roller coaster. That feeling was coming from this place I didn't recognize and I didn't understand. The inner workings of my thoughts and feelings created so much energy I was consistently wasting because I didn't know how to use it for my benefit. I had more energy than a little bit, and I was so confused. I once heard an amazing speaker say confused people do nothing, and that's exactly what I did, nothing.

I've never been much of a collector, but I recently realized that over the years, I've amassed an impressive collection of journals and notebooks. Attending conferences and workshops has always stirred up the gifts that were inside of me. My hands would move at a feverish pace to capture every golden nugget and insightful epitaph that was shared from the stage. I have filled countless notebooks with divine inspiration, million-dollar ideas, and grand *ah-ah*s, yet I still would do absolutely nothing with what I wrote. The pages of those beautifully decorated notebooks contained so much promise and possibility and untapped potential.

To be honest, if I were to go back and glean from those notebooks I've collected over the years, I would probably have a multi-million-dollar business strategy just from all the ideas that were inspired by things I heard.

My momentum moment happened when I finally made the connection that the fear I was feeling was creating energy, which must be converted for maximum benefit. My energy had to be channeled somewhere so I could do something with it. I realized I couldn't continue to create this much energy and not put it to good use. I made a decision to use this energy to do something every day to move my business forward. I took baby steps, and I was still terrified because doing nothing had become my comfort zone, and feeling forward motion in my business was unfamiliar to me.

Fear has power and a purpose. Its power can be converted to energy, but its purpose is an indicator you're close to something significant. Fear influences the way you think, and your thoughts motivate your behavior. When you understand the purpose of fear in your business, you'll see its value and benefit for creating motion and momentum. Every summer, I would go to one of my favorite theme parks, and I would make the daring decision to ride the newest, biggest, fastest, and scariest roller coaster in the park. I anticipated the thrill for weeks leading to the day I finally got a chance to ride the coaster. I have patiently waited in ridiculously long lines where I had plenty of time to think about how crazy and irrational this idea was and more importantly how to get myself out of the line. As I approached the station, I contemplated my exit strategy, my excuse for not going through with the very thing I was excited about and how I would handle the critics who would have an opinion about my decision to walk away.

With trepidation I would board into the car, and with hesitation, I would fasten my seatbelt then brace for the car to leave the station. As we would begin the slow ascent up the largest hill, my heart would race just as fast as my mind. Thoughts ranging from imminent doom all the way to eager anticipation and excitement would flow through my mind like water. The warning signs on the sides of the ride did nothing to calm my nerves, but the one sign that stood out the most to me was the one that read, "Smile for your photo."

Ugh. The dreaded roller coaster photo. The moment where momentum builds, forward motion is inevitable, and your stomach is dropping is the moment the engineers thought would make a great photo. Not when I was in line and excited. Not when I was poised and trying not to show my fear while boarding. And certainly not at the end of the ride when relief sets in. The photo is taken at the most terrifying moment. What exactly are they trying to prove here? As I looked at my photo, I noticed how desperately I was trying to smile and look like I had composure, but the reality was I didn't think I was going to make it.

When I made the decision to really build my business, it honestly felt just like boarding the roller coaster car in the station. I was excited and terrified at the same time. I made excuses in my mind and tried to talk myself out of it, but I did it anyway. That one decision to build it anyway created the forward motion and plugging into a system of support and positive input produced enough momentum for me to climb the initial hill. That hill consisted of properly establishing the structure of my business and hearing a bunch of nos. I couldn't quit if I wanted to because the amount of momentum with which I started had pushed me to the top of the hill. It was so critical that I kept my eyes forward because looking backward would have sent me backward—and fast.

There was a moment in starting my business that felt like the world's longest pregnant pause. My thoughts and fears began to catch up to the level of progress I had achieved, and it felt like everything around me was still. I was ready to move forward, but everything around me was at a standstill, and all of a sudden, the right connection came along and tipped my business in the right direction, and I was rolling at lightning speed. Somewhere between the pregnant pause and the strategic connection came the mental click of "Oh snap. This is happening," and eventually, I opened my eyes to really see, feel, and embrace what was ahead of me. It was in that moment that I realized this entrepreneurial journey and the thoughts and fears that come with it are not elements of theory, but instead they are laws of physics.

Fear is an energy producer that originates from your internal thoughts. In the same way that water produces energy that can be captured and turned into electricity, fear also produces energy that can be converted into power and leveraged for your business momentum.

So, if fear produces energy, then what is energy? Energy is a quantitative property that must be transferred to an object in order for it to perform work. So, what does this mean for you? You must put energy behind your business idea in order for it to work for you.

So, what is a quantitative property? A quantitative property is matter that can be observed and measured without changing its identity. So, what does this mean for you? Your business idea was good from the very beginning. You should be able to visualize your customers using your product or service and measure its profit potential without changing your original business idea. Although new information can help your original business idea evolve into something great, you can't allow the fear of not including everything to prevent you from doing something.

How do we convert fear into energy? Law of energy conservation tells us that energy can be converted in form, but not created or destroyed. Converting the energy produced by fear into an energy source for business momentum is not theory. It's physics. The fear lives in our thoughts and our thoughts give power to our actions.

The conversion of energy produced by fear happens between origination of your thought and the action you subsequently take. Let's practice this by completing the following sentence:

"When I think about (1) _____, I begin to feel fear of (2) _____, and as a result I do (3) _____."

The response you entered into the second (2) blank is a fear that is empowering the action you describe in the third (3) blank. The energy that is converted between the thought you share in the first (1) blank and the action you describe in the third (3) blank is either positive or negative. Positive energy creates forward business momentum. Negative energy does not move your business at all because no momentum was created.

What is momentum? Momentum is a physics term that describes mass in motion. How does this relate to your business? To gain momentum with your business idea, you must consistently take action to move forward.

What is motion? The law of motion says an object at rest stays at rest and an object in motion stays in motion unless acted upon by an unbalanced force. How does this relate to your business? This one is simple: A business idea in motion stays in motion until negative thoughts, distractions, or unforeseen circumstances interfere. A business idea written in a notebook stays in a notebook unless acted upon.

Positive energy is the most effective tool for creating your business momentum. Positive thinking deactivates the negative energy that is produced by fear. You must learn to recognize your fear in order to use the energy it produces for your own benefit. Identifying your thoughts and resulting actions can help change your perspective about your business and ultimately your business outcomes.

Who knew your thoughts and fears could have so much power? The fear lives in our thoughts, and our thoughts give power to our actions.

A FEW THOUGHTS FOR YOUR CONSIDERATION

What are you thinking about that's causing you to feel afraid of starting or growing your business?

_____
_____
_____
_____

How would you describe this fear?

_____
_____
_____
_____

What are you truly afraid of?

_____
_____
_____
_____

What actions are you taking, or decisions are you making, as a result of this fear?

_____
_____
_____
_____

CHAPTER EIGHT:

DISMANTLING LIMITING BELIEFS

Entrepreneurship has always been an aspirational dream of mine. For some reason, I could never muster enough courage to quit my day job and start a business. The beliefs I held on to about my ability to start and grow a successful business have always been tightly woven to my life experiences.

As a child, I lived through periods of homelessness, sleeping in the back of my mom's Pontiac Trans Am. We were often precariously housed, living with family members and my mom's friends. This created an underlying fear of housing instability. As I grew older, I knew I never wanted the pursuit of my dreams to result in my family and me not having our own home. And as a young mom, I wanted to ensure my child never went through the things I experienced.

I did everything I could to create a life of stability for her—the sacrifice was great, but the reward was even greater.

For years, I lived my life by the mantra, "Get a good education, a good job, and do the best you can." However, this was a mantra for a life of mediocrity. It was my belief the only way to truly make it was to work a job, so I focused on my professional development to stabilize my career. By immersing myself in lifelong learning and getting as many certifications as I could, I invested significant amounts of time and money into ensuring I remained employed and could provide for my child. I was completely sold out to the idea of being a stellar employee because, in my mind, living paycheck to paycheck was safer than pursuing my dreams of entrepreneurship.

The toughest part about this small glimpse into my past is not the fear of being homeless, underlying worries, or financial woes, but the fact that I was willing to invest so much of myself to become the best employee only to live my life just over broke (J.O.B). How different my life could have been if I had only dedicated that same energy to believing in my knowledge, skills, and abilities to become a successful business owner.

After years of toying with the idea of entrepreneurship, I had an encounter with a friend who basically told me hiding my light is not how I was meant to serve the world. She reminded me I couldn't accomplish anything by hiding in the shadows of my underlying fears. The only way to release my light and move forward into entrepreneurship was to do the necessary work to capture my limiting beliefs and dismantle the thoughts that were no longer serving me. My friend suggested I get a notebook and start journaling. I wasn't interested.

In my mind, the highest and best use of a beautiful notebook was to take it with me to conferences and trainings where I would write notes—notes that I would never use and all the great ideas I would never carry out. I was not the girl who could just sit and pour out her heart on the pages of a journal. The day after her suggestion, I went to lunch with another friend who wanted to meet because she had a gift for me. Even though it wasn't my birthday, I was excited she thought enough about me to give me a gift. Guess what the gift was? A journal. Not just any journal. This journal had a special message on it the front that read, *Perhaps this is the moment for which you have been created.* I sunk to the bottom of my chair and began to cry.

You see, the friend who suggested I start journaling doesn't know the friend who gave me the journal. To this day, these two women have never spoken and never met. Both women believed in me, even when I wasn't convinced I believed in myself. A collision of destiny was happening, and I couldn't deny what I was supposed to do.

It's funny how we ask for a sign to validate our decision or to confirm we're on the right track, and when the sign does finally come, we question everything about it. Something about this time was different. The belief that my friends had in my ability to be successful invalidated my excuses.

My whole life, I studied at the school of hard knocks, and I earned a master's degree in urban survival and how to just get by. What I didn't learn was how to move beyond survival into thriving. I knew how to be an exceptional employee and a diligent learner, but I didn't know how to trust myself, my faith, or my unique value enough to successfully start and grow a business.

I remember lying in bed one night crying and speaking out loud all of my fears—fear of failing and succeeding, concerns of financial hardship, fear of abundance, fear of instability, and fear of being alone. As I lay there with my emotions leaking all over my pillow, a comforting peace came over me. It was at that moment that I realized I had everything I needed to be successful. All the training, certifications, and professional development throughout the years prepared me for this moment. I stopped rehearsing all the negative things that could go wrong if I were to lose my consistent paycheck, my current home, or even a few friends.

I remembered something my mom said to me when I was afraid to run for the president position in my youth group. I was adamant about my reason for not running for the seat. I gave my mom every excuse I could think of, and although I had a ton of great ideas, I still didn't believe anyone would vote for me. I told her I decided not to run because I didn't want anyone to see me lose.

My mom looked at me over the top of her tinted eyeglasses with a lit Kool Filter King cigarette in one hand and a Coca-Cola Classic in the other. After blowing the cigarette smoke over her shoulder, she turned to me and said, "Oh my baby, what if you win?"

I hadn't thought about the idea of me winning. I was more afraid of people seeing me lose than I was of actually trying to win. Because my mom believed in me, I added my name to the ballot and won. I served as president of that organization from ages eleven to seventeen when I left for college. The echo of my mother's voice was a seed that planted a new way of thinking about my old fears. The same belief that propelled me to get over my fears and run for office was the same belief that produced the energy I needed to write my letter of resignation to leave my full-time job and become a full-time entrepreneur.

I didn't ease into entrepreneurship; I pole vaulted. The month that passed between the day I gave my notice up until my last day on the job was spent building the foundational elements of my business. I was utterly terrified the entire time. I believed I would give my absolute best effort to every client I had the honor to serve. I believed my knowledge, skills, and abilities were sufficient to make a difference and that what I didn't know could be learned. I believed my services were valuable and that I deserved the price listed on the invoice and more. It was the positive energy created by these beliefs that made me courageous enough to launch. Unpacking my limiting beliefs was the beginning stage of my transformation from employee to entrepreneur. For you, I would encourage you to dig deep to uncover which beliefs are hidden under your decision to not act. Let us practice this idea here in the book or in your favorite notebook. First, analyze your thoughts about you as a business owner. Compete the following:

When I think about myself as a full-time business owner, I think about …

_____

_____

_____

_____

Next, create a list of your negative and limiting beliefs as well as your positive productive beliefs about yourself as a business owner.

Negative Thoughts & Beliefs	Positive Thoughts & Beliefs

For both the positive and negative, spend a little time reflecting on which of your life experiences most likely contributed to the development of these beliefs and what has the resulting outcome been, and make note of your responses. Finally, make a list of ten things you can do today only using the things you currently have that can move you closer to the start of your business.

1. _____

2. _____

3. _____

4. _____

5. _____

6. _____

7. _____

8. _____

9. _____

10. _____

Completing this exercise in the notebook given to me by my friend is how I began to move beyond my negative and limiting beliefs and toward creating a positive and productive plan of action for my business.

Your plan for your business is an indicator of how you intend to build and ultimately run your business. Many external factors contribute to your ability to operate according to plan. While a plan is a very necessary part of the development and launch process, you must believe in your ability to execute the plans you have written. The truth is an entrepreneur with a weak plan on paper can still successfully build a multi-million-dollar company if they believe in their ability to do so.

In the same way, an entrepreneur with a really strong plan on paper can completely fail at business and shutter their doors just as quickly as they opened them when their belief and confidence are low. Your beliefs represent your trust, faith, or confidence in someone or something. It is your personal attitude about whether an idea or thought is true.

If you believe you have the creativity, focus, and discipline to solve any problem that comes up in your business, then that will come true. On the other hand, if you believe there's no room left for your ideas or that you'll never be able to lead other people toward your vision, that will also come true.

Developing healthy thought habits is an essential contributor to your success as an entrepreneur. Create your own positive affirmations for business growth and speak them out loud daily. This routine will become a habit, and this habit will eventually become your beliefs. You may say things like:

"I have what it takes to start and grow a successful business."

"Loyal and appreciative customers are attracted to my business daily."

"I am worthy of financial success."

"My business adds value to my customers, my community, and my family."

" _____ "

" _____ "

" _____ "

Everything about your business will thrive when you believe in the positive impact it will have on your future, your community, and the lives of your customers. When you believe your business can and will make a difference and a profit, you'll work harder, give more, and apply the level of energy and passion that is essential to creating anything great. I know we all want to believe we're building a phenomenal business that will have a tremendous success rate, innovate, disrupt, and change the world. The only way to make this happen is to convert our beliefs into action and work until it becomes a reality. Naturally, your commitment, discipline, and focus to build your business grows when your belief in what you're building remains high. Positive beliefs about yourself create positive energy in your business.

CHAPTER NINE:

THE MOTIVATION TO KEEP GOING

Entrepreneurship is like the fairytale romance that everyone dreams of but only a few people ever experience. The allure of freedom to set your own schedule and to take charge of your own professional destiny sends your imagination on a wild ride. The whimsy of doing what you love and loving what you do every single day fuels your passion to pursue your dream. The promise of financial stability and endless growth opportunity draws you in to embrace your potential. The idea that you'll build your dream business and live happily ever after is easy to fall in love with. In reality, entrepreneurship is no fairytale. It takes hard work, consistent effort, self-motivation, and determination to turn your dream into a successful and profitable business venture. Getting motivated to start a business is easy. Staying motivated can be a bit more challenging. During the dream phase of entrepreneurship, motivation is abundantly overflowing. During the building phase, your motivation can quickly subside as the pre-launch task list steadily grows.

Where does entrepreneurial motivation come from? Entrepreneurial motivation is influenced by intrinsic and extrinsic factors. The intrinsic factors include independence, autonomy, and self-actualization. The extrinsic factors include increased personal income, respect from peers, and an elevated economic standing.

Your ability to maintain motivation is essential for your business success. The core of all motivation is in your thoughts, which is why it is so vitally important to maintain healthy positive thoughts. If motivation produces the energy necessary to take productive action, then that means your thoughts can and will do the same. In order to leverage the energy created by motivation, you must develop healthy thought habits. Try things like saving motivational quotes as your screen saver on electronic devices or as artwork on your walls. Find motivational videos on streaming sites from people you admire, and have conversations with other business owners who have achieved the level of success you desire. Staying motivated will be beneficial to you and your customers.

Every entrepreneur experiences the occasional slump. Sometimes you're just fresh out of new ideas, you may be burnt out from burning the midnight oil, or maybe things just aren't working out the way you imagined they would. Negative thoughts and doubts can easily creep in when you're going through a low period in your business. Regardless of how things may seem to be going, your ability to self-motivate plays a tremendous role in turning things around for you. Keep in mind that even after a setback, motivation can help you to take your thoughts captive and seek out the solutions that will get you back on track. Regaining motivation is key to your comeback.

When you're low on motivation, it's important that you have resources in place to help you to mentally bounce back. Trying to build a business with low motivation is like trying to run a marathon with low energy. You will quickly burn out. Low motivation can create a nonchalant attitude toward your work and cause missed deadlines, avoidable mistakes, lost opportunities, and ultimately lost revenue.

If you struggle to maintain motivation, know you aren't alone. Many entrepreneurs struggle with this very thing. Take a moment to gather your thoughts and surround yourself with positive things that motivate you to keep going. Something so simple as listening to a motivational message or reading the story of a business owner who has overcome can give you the extra boost you need to keep going. Just don't give up.

The key to achieving lasting entrepreneurial success is in the way you think about your business. Here are a few things you can do to stay motivated as an entrepreneur:

Take notes from your heroes. Success leaves clues. Many of the people you admire in business have written books or openly share about their journey on social platforms. Listen. Study. Observe. Only apply what you need. Your story is unique to you, so resist the temptation to imitate their actions.

Set your mind on things that are positive. If it's true, good, and it adds value to you and others, it's probably a great point of focus. Remember, everyone's journey is different. Don't get caught up in the paradox of comparison. It will rob you of your joy.

Remember to have fun. Starting a business doesn't have to be all work and no play. While this journey can be stressful, it can also be fun. Enjoy the process of creating the business of your dreams.

Clearly write out your plans. When you do this, you inadvertently create a map for your goals. Having your plans written clearly gives you a big-picture view of what you desire to accomplish, and it allows you to break it down into measurable steps.

Celebrate the little wins along the way. Properly setting your business structure is huge. Celebrate it. Just because anybody can do it doesn't mean everybody will do it, but you did, so celebrate it. You can and will accomplish so many amazing things on this journey. Enjoy it.

There are a million ways to stay motivated, but all you need is one. Get clear on the vision you have for your life and your business and hold on to that. When fear and doubt creep in and try to rob you of your joy, remember your vision and review your plan. This will allow you to tap into the original motivation that started you on the journey of entrepreneurship to begin with. Everything you need to sustain the motivation to succeed is in your thoughts. Stay positive, and defy the urge to quit.

 # A FEW THOUGHTS FOR YOUR CONSIDERATION

How do you stay motivated to build your business?

_____

_____

_____

What do you do to lift your mood when you begin to lose confidence in your business?

_____

_____

_____

_____

After reading this chapter, what will you do differently to maintain your motivation?

_____

_____

_____

_____

PART FOUR: FINALLY ENJOY THE RIDE

CHAPTER TEN:

CONVERTING NERVOUS ENERGY

For years, I imagined what life for me would be like as an entrepreneur. I imagined the freedom to be my own boss, make my own decisions, and the ability to create solutions I believed would have the greatest impact. Throughout my career, I held positions that were entrepreneurial adjacent, meaning the role allowed for creative autonomy for development but implementation required several layers of approvals and signatures. My last traditional job before starting my business was helping business owners navigate the process of properly launching their business in a new market. To celebrate their success, I would coordinate with the local officials to have the mayor officiate a ribbon-cutting ceremony. My role was ensuring the business was in good standing, to schedule the event, and accompany the mayor to the celebration with giant scissors and commemorative ribbon.

Before each event, I would polish the scissors to remove all fingerprints and to make sure the moment felt special when the business owner would pick the giant scissors up for the very first time. Standing there and being present during these special celebrations brought about feelings of joy and a dull, aching desire to take the leap and start my own company. I'll never forget the week leading up to my last day on the job. I flipped through hundreds of ribbon-cutting photos and reflected on each business owner's journey leading up to that big day. The memories gave me peace and reassurance that hard work and determination will get the door open.

I grabbed the ceremonial scissors from the velvet-lined case, took them in my hands, and with warm tears rolling down my cheeks, I polished those scissors one last time. You see,

I knew the next time my hands touched those scissors, it would be at the ribbon-cutting celebration for my business.

Opening day of anything can be incredibly exciting. There is a tremendous amount of nervous energy that's generated when you're preparing to officially introduce your business to the world. This nervousness can cause you to lose sleep. Sometimes you can't eat, and don't even think about trying to focus. It becomes impossible to focus because your mind is racing everywhere, and the nervous energy continuously builds as the clock slowly ticks away to the moment you'll officially announce to everyone you're open for business.

Like fear, nervousness can produce energy that's either positive or negative. Positive nervous energy is productive, and negative nervous energy is non-productive. Converting positive nervous energy into productive energy gives you the power to handle and manage a ton of logistical details while still taking everything in stride. If nervous energy is converted into non-productive and negative energy, you feel practically frozen in place. You may even experience crying spells, racing thoughts, or self-doubt. This pattern of thinking can be completely disruptive to your overall progress.

It is very normal for entrepreneurs who are courageous and brave enough start a business to get to opening day and to have feelings of uncertainty rush in and rob them of an otherwise joyous moment. You totally earned every moment of your celebration, especially after the countless hours of building a website, creating business cards, not to mention perfecting your product or service.

It is possible to have total confidence in knowing the world had a problem only your business and your unique approach could solve, but when you get to opening day, all of a sudden, it feels like everyone in the world knows so much more than you. Despite all the evidence that says you're experienced, talented, and most importantly qualified to successfully run this business, you begin to doubt your own ability, and you become terrified of what people will think of your work.

People will judge you. People will question whether they think you're good enough. People will even question your credentialing, the number of plaques you have on the wall, and the very letters behind your name. You validate people when you allow their unjustly judgmental and hyper-critical sentiments to question your own worthiness to hang a shingle that says open. When these non-productive thoughts and fears created by negative nervous energy creep in, you must take those thoughts captive. When you do this, you can take their power by converting that nervous energy into beneficial actions that work to your advantage. You can do this by simply changing the way you think about your valuable business, your unique skills, and your demonstrated abilities.

Unconverted nervous energy can and will infiltrate the very fiber of the business and work counterproductively against everything you created. If you work diligently to change your thoughts about your ability to successfully run a business, you will harness the power and energy necessary to provide quality service to your clients and to leave a lasting impression of excellence.

When I think about the day of the ribbon-cutting celebration for my business, I remember feeling excited and terrified at the same time. I personally invited about thirty friends, family members, and local colleagues to celebrate with me. To make the day extra special, I rented an event venue and covered the room with my unique branding so that every picture reflected the day. I prepared a delicious spread of my favorite foods and even hired a designer to make a dress especially for me, which I'd never done before, but I wanted to make sure I looked as special as I felt. I hired a professional makeup artist to do my makeup because that's definitely not my gifting. I also hired a professional photographer to come and take pictures to capture the moments of that special day.

Needless to say, I went all out for this special moment in my life. I was ready. I was super excited. I was psyched—or at least I thought I was. As the hour drew near the official ribbon cutting, I realized I was going to have to talk to people about my business and tell them what I do. I didn't want to talk to anyone about my business. I just wanted to celebrate the fact that it was open. There. I did it. I checked the box of full-time entrepreneur. Surely that was enough, right? Wrong.

I'm not afraid of the stage, and I honestly enjoy public speaking, but the thought of talking to people about my business made me nervous. I really just wanted to do the work and show everyone how awesome my business was without explaining what I actually did. The truth is, I was afraid of judgment and people questioning my ability to do a good job. The thought of someone speaking badly about something I was so passionate about scared me. My nervousness got so bad I longed for the logistical hiccups that would allow me to run behind the scenes and hide for a bit. I was so grateful for these moments because it took my mind away from how nervous I really was.

When the mayor, the Chamber of Commerce, and the Economic Development Authority arrived, I was so excited and so proud because earlier in my career I was one of them. I was the person who showed up at every event with the neatly polished scissors and a giant roll of ribbon, and now finally, it was my turn. I got to stand at the front of the room, and someone was hosting a ribbon cutting ceremony for me.

Remembering that moment still takes my breath away. I could not stop smiling. My face literally hurt, and my cheek muscles were tight from smiling. Tears were flowing down my face, and I felt every drop as it hit my chin. I couldn't believe this moment was finally here.

Then it happened, we cut the ribbon, and everyone cheered. I hugged the mayor and scanned the room to take in the moment, and I suddenly realized the group of thirty people I had personally invited was actually closer to two hundred attendees. There were so many people who were actually happy for me and who wanted to celebrate this milestone with me. They saw something in me all along I didn't even see in myself. I was afraid of judgment, but instead, I was overwhelmed with gratitude and completely humbled by support. I couldn't believe so many people had showed up to celebrate the grand opening of my business with me.

Taking my thoughts captive helped me to realize that nervous energy I was feeling wasn't because I was afraid to tell people about my business. I was afraid of being judged or criticized by the people who doubted my ability. I had a strong desire to make a great first impression. I wanted to say the right words in the right way to make people think I would be incredibly successful no matter what I did.

Here is the lesson in this: You must first determine the source or the root of the nervous energy. When you determine the source, you can capture the thought. When you capture the thought, you can identify ways to change your business development behavior and ultimately your business outcomes. What you think about your business really does impact your outcomes. If you think things like, *No one will buy from me,* then your actions will support that thought by procrastinating on related growth activities.

Rejection is real, but it isn't always personal. Perhaps a person isn't in the market to buy what you're selling today. If you convert the non-productive negative energy created by nervousness into a beneficial thought, you'll quickly realize that individual's potential to be a great referral resource for you. This can still result in a win for your business. You must quit taking rejection personally in order to clearly see new opportunities. Replace the captive thought of *I can't. I got another no* with the more productive thought of *I am so proud I bravely took action to have a conversation with another human being about my unique approach to solving a very real problem.*

You have the power to naturally convert nervousness into a viable productive and positive energy source to move your business forward. Focus on what you know is true about your knowledge, experience, and unique qualifications.

Knowing you have the ability to change your business outcomes by simply changing the way you think is your most valuable asset. Strive to bring your thoughts and behavior into alignment with where you see your business going next.

A FEW THOUGHTS FOR YOUR CONSIDERATION

What non-productive, negative, and nervous energy creating thoughts do I need to take captive in order to share my business story?

_____

_____

_____

_____

I am knowledgeable and experienced in _____ .

I am so uniquely skilled in _____ **that I am building a successful business.**

CHAPTER ELEVEN: A LITTLE BIT OF

GRATITUDE GOES A LONG WAY

Absolutely no one is self-made. Even though you're in business for yourself, you are never alone. The growth process that comes with starting a business can feel extremely lonely, and that's normal. When you start down the path of entrepreneurship, you'll find very few people understand what you're experiencing. Some will distance themselves to allow you space to create. Others leave because they can no longer relate to you, or they may even be a little envious of the fact that you're courageous enough to start the thing they could only dream of.

When you look around, notice you're surrounded by people who have a vested interest in seeing you win, and for that, you should be grateful. For some, it's your family members who have cheered you on and who have adjusted to ensure you succeed. For others, it's friends who are functioning as your personal pep squad and keeping your spirits high as you build. It may be your community that's rallying around you to be a great business owner. You may even have vendors who believe in you and your business so much they offer you exclusive deals and share valuable resources just to help you grow. There's only one emotional response appropriate for this type of support, and that's gratitude.

Gratus is a Latin word meaning *heartwarming, nice, pleasing,* and *thankful.* Showing gratitude is an expression of thanks and appreciation for what someone has done for you, along with the results their act of kindness produced for you and your business. Gratitude is recognizing the person didn't have to do anything for you, but because they chose to, you are grateful. Gratitude is a state of mind that is rich with intrinsic and extrinsic benefits.

Intrinsically, expressing gratitude can:

- greatly improve physical and mental health.

- boost self-esteem.

- enhance empathy and resilience.

Extrinsically, expressing gratitude can:

- strengthen relationships.

- build trust and rapport.

- improve your reputation as a leader.

Expressing gratitude when business is good and all seems right with the world is easy. But when business is a challenge and things are not working the way you had hoped they would, expressing gratitude feels impossible. Authenticity and a genuine heart are essential. No matter what you may be going through, it's important to make time and reflect on positive, true, and good things. What you think and the words that come from your mouth all have an effect on how you ultimately feel about yourself, your business, and others.

Gratitude creates the type of energy that is highly contagious because it's directly reflected through your attitude. When you lack gratitude, you give off negative energy, and your mind is magnetically drawn to problems. This increases the likelihood of you giving up on your dreams of entrepreneurship prematurely. Set your mind on positive things, and soon, you will see all the people and things for which you should be grateful. The positive energy created by gratitude can be easily converted into a resource to build value-adding relationships that will help your business grow.

With intentional focus and effort, gratitude can become a mental habit. To develop any habit, you'll need to practice consistently, so make gratitude an essential part of your daily routine. Start by going back to the basics and use the words *please* and *thank you* with everyone you encounter. Find something good in every challenging situation. Focusing on the positive helps to reduce stress and increase your productivity.

Relationships are so important in every area of your business. As an entrepreneur, you must prioritize nurturing the relationships that matter in your life and business. Verbal expressions of gratitude with a simple *thank you* and written expressions of gratitude via email or a handwritten note elevate the quality of your relationship with the people who matter most.

Strong professional relationships lead to referred business and vital industry connections that can help your business scale and grow. Send a follow-up email to new contacts within twenty-four hours of networking events and social activities. Invite them for an additional conversation by phone or in person. Genuinely show interest in learning more about the person with whom you're meeting and their business. Thank them sincerely and often for their time and any offers to help you and your business.

Solid customer relationships directly impact your bottom line. Learn about your customer by immersing yourself in their world. Socialize in the same places as your ideal target market. Make connections by serving the community and giving back. You can also try to remember customer names, birthdays, and other unique things about them. This shows your customers they matter enough for you to remember little details. Again, thank them sincerely and often.

The most valuable relationships of all are with your family and friends. Make time for telling them how much you appreciate them. Schedule milestones, major events, and a few activities on your calendar to help you remember to acknowledge them and support when you can. Your friends and family want to know you won't grow into an overnight success and forget all about them. Once more, thank them sincerely and often to show your gratitude and appreciation for their love and support.

 # A FEW THOUGHTS FOR YOUR CONSIDERATION

Who are you thankful for helping you along in your entrepreneurial journey?

_____
_____
_____
_____

What resources are you thankful for?

_____
_____
_____
_____

CHAPTER TWELVE:

GAINING CONFIDENCE

Entrepreneurship is the adrenaline rush of a lifetime. With its peaks and valleys, twists and turns, I highly recommend you try it at least once in your life. After you've experienced the full emotional roller coaster of entrepreneurship, the thrill becomes addictive, and you'll find yourself seeking more and more business opportunities. Every emotion you feel—from excited through doubt—is all necessary to build your tolerance to handle the highs and lows of business.

I wish I could tell you the butterfly-in-your-stomach feeling eventually fades, but it never does. The bigger the risk, the more flutters you'll feel. Learn to embrace the fluttery butterfly feeling as a natural indicator you're about to embark on an incredibly exhilarating journey that will lead to profitability if you hang in there. As your tolerance for riding the emotional coaster builds, so will your entrepreneurial confidence.

The confidence you have as an entrepreneur is closely related to self-confidence in that they are both intrinsically connected to how you think and feel about you and your abilities. Self-confidence describes your attitude toward your skills and the level of trust you have in your abilities. Positive self-confidence creates the energy necessary to put your business idea on paper and to speak with a manner of authority about your business to others. Negative self-confidence creates a lingering energy that creeps in when you least expect it and creates a weighted sensation that slows your progress and drags you down. Positive self-confidence is the framework of your coaster and your business. It must be present and tested for stability before anything lucrative can be applied.

Your entrepreneurial confidence describes your attitude and beliefs about your ability to actually run a business of your own and the level of trust you have in your ability to turn a profit. You may be totally gifted in generating business ideas, forming the legal structure, and developing the brand identity, yet still lack confidence in your ability to run the business successfully. This is totally normal. If you are the type of person who is constantly creating new business concepts and have yet to profit from a single idea, you may be lacking entrepreneurial confidence. Just like self-confidence, entrepreneurial confidence can create both positive and negative energy.

If you have positive entrepreneurial confidence, you'll build the business, present it to the marketplace, and champion your brand to potential customers. The energy generated by positive entrepreneurial confidence fuels your passion when discussing your product or service as a viable solution to challenges in the market. Negative entrepreneurial confidence creates an energy that will turn you into a wallflower at networking events and will cause your mind to go blank when delivering your elevator pitch to prospects. Understanding your level of entrepreneurial confidence and how it's impacting your launch can help you shift from stagnation to momentum.

Why would anyone else believe in you if you don't believe in yourself? Now, I know there may be times where friends or family members encourage us to start a business because they believe we would be really successful if we sold _____ or if we started a _____ business. While their encouragement can be exciting, you know that it's going to take a lot more than their words to start a business. If your confidence isn't there, your business won't be either. Your family and friends can want entrepreneurship for you more than you want it for yourself. Entrepreneur doubt produces consumer doubt, and that's just bad for business. Entrepreneurs who lack confidence are at the mercy of their own limiting thoughts. If you think you're going to be a failure in business, you will be. However, if you think you'll be successful in business, you will be. Your business will always grow in the direction of your thoughts.

If you're like most aspiring entrepreneurs, you may find you're high on ideas and low on entrepreneurial confidence. Again, let me assure you this is totally normal. The key is to be honest with yourself. Low confidence is not an indication of a lost cause. Instead, it is an opportunity to build your confidence and strengthen your level of trust in your own abilities. Try these three techniques to build your entrepreneurial confidence:

1. **Conduct a Personal SWOT Analysis.** A SWOT analysis is a technique used to help you identify your

strengths, weaknesses, opportunities, and threats related to building a business.

2. **Watch Your Mouth.**

- Be mindful of the words you speak and the thoughts you entertain about your ability to run a successful business.

- Create a new mantra and verbally repeat it daily. Try saying something like this out loud while looking at yourself in the mirror: "I am a successful, resilient, and innovative entrepreneur. I attract loyal customers who willingly invest in my products and services. I am worthy of generating revenue. I have the knowledge, skill, and ability to be successful in everything I set out to do."

3. **Sell Something.**

- Nothing boosts your entrepreneurial confidence like making a sale.

- Begin with pre-sales, pre-orders, or pre-paid offers from customers who want to support your business. You'll be less likely to quit when you know people are financially invested in your launch.

Aspiring entrepreneurs who are insecure and afraid will wallow in their comfort zone. They stand by and watch business happen from the spectator bridge under the highest point of the coaster. It's more profitable to be in business than it is to think about business. Just like roller coasters, entrepreneurship is not for the faint of heart. It takes courage and boldness to even think about becoming an entrepreneur. If entrepreneurship were easy, everyone would do it. When you make the decision to start a business, be confident in knowing no one gets to skip the line or bypass the emotional roller coaster of entrepreneurship. Climb into the front seat with confidence and excitement about your new venture. Think of the first obstacle you face as a hill that can be leveraged to gain momentum and not an indicator to quit.

All new entrepreneurs will endure the occasional pitfall that will expose areas of weakness. Learn and take notes on the lessons that each twist, turn, and loop teaches you. This will be helpful as you go forward.

Finally, remember to enjoy the ride. Be confident in your ability to conceptualize, strategize, and actualize a business. Be willing to take risks. Be openminded and flexible. Learn to convert the energy created by your emotions into fuel for forward momentum so you can conquer the emotional roller coaster of entrepreneurship. Just because entrepreneurship is scary doesn't mean that it can't be fun.

A FEW THOUGHTS FOR YOUR CONSIDERATION

What are your personal strengths?

_____

_____

_____

_____

What are your professional strengths?

_____

_____

_____

_____

How will these strengths help you as an entrepreneur?

_____

_____

_____

_____

What are your personal weaknesses?

_____

_____

_____

_____

What are your professional weaknesses?

_____

_____

_____

_____

How might these weaknesses hinder you as an entrepreneur?

_____

_____

_____

_____

Describe the personal and professional opportunities that will be created for you by becoming an entrepreneur.

_____

_____

_____

_____

Describe the personal and professional opportunities you might miss if you became an entrepreneur.

_____

_____

_____

_____

How can these opportunities be leveraged for your entrepreneurial advantage?

_____

_____

_____

_____

What are the known or perceived threats to you personally that will result from starting a business?

_____

_____

_____

_____

What are any known or perceived threats to you professionally that will result from starting a business?

_____

_____

_____

_____

How can the knowledge or awareness of these threats be used to your entrepreneurial advantage?

_____

_____

_____

_____

CONCLUSION

The frame of the roller coaster represents the path we must follow in order to get our businesses started. There as many paths to starting a business as there are roller coasters in the world. You are not limited to one. You have a choice. Don't allow your emotions to be the decision maker of which path to starting you choose.

The car represents the business idea that you will introduce to the market. In the same way that you can't safely ride in multiple roller coaster cars at the same time, you should not attempt to introduce all of your business ideas at the same time. You are welcome to ride that coaster multiple times, choosing a different car for each ride, but you will have to go through the entire process each time. Don't try to skip steps. You will increase your ability to gain emotional control and reduce stress if you avoid overcomplicating the process of simply starting.

The other passengers on the train with you represent the myriad of emotions that will be a part of your journey. It is rare that you will ride a roller coaster and you are the only passenger. Each passenger that boards the train is bringing their own emotional baggage along with them. Imagine if you felt their emotions all at the same time, it would probably be overwhelming. Emotions will be present in the process of starting your business. It is important to remember that you should only try and process the one at a time.

Just like riding a roller coaster, you will experience some topsy-turvy times but if you stay the course you can conquer any emotion that presents itself as a barrier to achieving your entrepreneurial goals.

There aren't enough words to express my sincere gratitude to you for reading my book. Time is one of life's most precious gifts, and I hope you feel your time was well spent. I genuinely believe that when we develop a better understanding of our own thoughts and emotions, we become free from emotional bondage and we can conquer anything.

As you reflect to some parts of this book, I would like for you to consider sharing those thoughts with a friend or fellow entrepreneur who could benefit from them. In conclusion, I leave you with these thoughts:

1) **Learn to enjoy the ride.** It's really hard to enjoy the experience when your emotions seem to be running away from you.

2) **Every emotion you feel on your entrepreneurial journey is valid, real, and present for a reason.** Pay attention to it and learn from it. When you have learned

why the emotion is present, where it is coming from, and how can you leverage it to move your business forward, then you can enjoy the ride.

3) **Open your eyes to get a clearer perspective of what's ahead of you.** You'll miss all the special moments along the way if you make moves with your eyes closed.

4) **Throw your hands in the air and release the things you can't control or influence.** Sometimes we'll hold on to ideas, connections, and resources that no longer serve us when we should just let go.

5) **Feel confident and secure in knowing that you are divinely held.** All good things will work in your favor.

6) **Be present in each moment.** Know that everything you need is already inside of you, so there is no need to be anxious.

I believe in you. The world is waiting for you to launch your business. Trust and believe that you will succeed.

A PERSONAL NOTE FROM MY DAUGHTER

To My Mother:

You are my hero who wears a cross instead of a cape. I've watched you overcome many trials in my life. I've watched you move mountains with the help of God. I've watched you make the impossible work. You have a superpower you only ever hear of moms having. Writing this book will not only help others on their journey to success, but it will be another thing that I already knew you could do. Thank you for all of the nights you stayed up fighting battles so I wouldn't have to. You deserve all of the success that is going to continue coming your way. This will be the book that will lead millions to successful businesses.

Love,

Z

AN INSPIRING POEM FROM A FRIEND

The Leap...

(Written by Simply Stacy for Kindra Dionne)

Stand tall,
You will not fall
You know you have the capability
To accomplish
It all
Nothing can stop you... but you
So, what are you going to do?
To see the manifestation of what is in you
Take the leap... the net
Will appear
It is OK to cry the tears
Navigate through the fears
Breathing backward, counting from ten
You can do this, you will win
The ride, yes, it is bumpy
The road ahead makes you jumpy
You have been equipped with everything
To stand with the victory in the middle of the ring
Take the leap... the net
Will appear
You trained for this
Endured the rain for this
Opportunities will pass
But the opportunity for you...
You will NOT miss
Step one, step two
Do this, for no one else
But Y O U
Be proud
Celebrate too

You took the leap
The net has appeared
Just for you!

ABOUT THE AUTHOR

Kindra Dionne is a visionary Business Development Consultant, Speaker and Author whose focus is on empowering entrepreneurs to thrive in an ever-changing business world. With over 15 years' experience, she is fueled by a passion for ensuring mission-driven entrepreneurs enter new markets with excellence so they can make a dollar and a difference.

Kindra is the President and CEO of Purpose WorX, LLC, a consulting firm that guides businesses through the process of strategizing, organizing, and actualizing their goals. She lends her expertise to entrepreneurs to enable them to launch new concepts with confidence by conquering business challenges and embracing strategic connections.

Besides work, Kindra enjoys reading business books that inspire her and playing with her dog Teddy.

Whether you are looking for a complete business transformation or a nudge to forge forward, you can count on Kindra to guide you in your exponential growth.

Made in the USA
Columbia, SC
31 October 2020